shine
your
icy
crown

amanda lovelace

shine
your
icy
crown

amanda lovelace

Andrews McMeel
PUBLISHING®

books by amanda lovelace

the

series:

the princess saves herself in this one (#1)
the witch doesn't burn in this one (#2)
the mermaid's voice returns in this one (#3)

slay those dragons: a journal for writing your own story

believe in your own magic: a 45-card oracle deck & guidebook

***

the
things that h(a)unt
duology:

to make monsters out of girls (#1)
to drink coffee with a ghost (#2)

***

the
you are your own fairy tale
series:

break your glass slippers (#1)
shine your icy crown (#2)

for every girl
who's ever been called a bitch
for speaking her mind.

so, like, every girl.

contents

a note from the author

welcome, dear reader! you see, the imagination is a funny, often elusive beast. the poetry collection you're about to read was inspired by several icy & witchy tales—both old & new, both familiar & perhaps unfamiliar. ultimately, though, i consider this to be an entirely new fairy tale of its own. while it *is* fiction, each poem is still nonetheless based on my own experiences in one way or another, especially the unique relationship between the two main characters.

here, sisters make up a large part of the magic.

but that's the case so much of the time, isn't it?

laced with love,
amanda

let me tell you a rebellious story

there is a girl who
loves fairy tales
more than anything,

but she doesn't
understand why
the princess's story

comes to a close
once she marries
the prince.

"what happens after?"
she wonders aloud,
but no one ever seems
to have an answer.

*let me tell you an even more
rebellious story*

there is a girl who
loves fairy tales
more than anything,

but no matter
how hard she searches
for an answer,

she can't understand
why there even
needs to be a prince.

"why doesn't the princess just
marry herself?" she asks,
to which they all reply,
"but that wouldn't be *romantic*."

i

once there lived a very stubborn princess who rejected every crown her father—a highly formidable king—presented her with, each of them crafted from the finest materials. however, that didn't stop her from waving them away without so much as a second look. none of them felt quite *right*. not long after, the rumors began to spread. it was believed widely that the princess had no love for tradition or for the kingdom or its people. some speculated her heart had been replaced with nothingness. at night, the princess's weeping could be heard all throughout the land, even deep within the forest, where only the tree spirits could hear.

they slept the way otters do—
holding hands, so as never to lose the other.

—*sisters.*

big sister says

i love you more than the moon above us. i love you more than
ursa minor & ursa major combined. i love you more than each
& every one of the stars. i love you more than the entire galaxy
& all of the galaxies they have yet to discover. you, too, are a
magnificent, celestial being. i can't imagine *not* being in the
same sky as you.

when she daydreams, she's never sitting beside the one who rules—no, she's always the one who does the ruling. along the way, someone comes up to her & tells her that women aren't mighty enough to do it all on their own. just like that, all her hopes crack & splinter, & she never sees the world the same way again.

—*patriarchy.*

big sister says

when other people choose not
to believe in your magic,

you must take it upon yourself to
believe in your *own* magic.

there will be no greater satisfaction
than proving them wrong.

i. "behave yourself."
ii. "don't ask questions."
iii. "cross your legs."
iv. "dress modestly."
v. "be seen, not heard."

—*the king & queen.*

big sister says

break the rules whenever you find the chance. live a life so fierce, bold, & carefree that people often accuse you of being a witch. you see, society fears nothing more than a woman who's not only aware of her power but also not afraid to use it in any way she sees fit. what could be more fun than constantly keeping them on their toes?

when she tells on him for yanking on both of her braids, they rush over to see whether *he* is okay. "we don't believe he would ever do such a thing," they tell her, ignoring her when she tries to explain the truth. *why does he always get away with everything?* she thinks. *no one ever believes me. it's not fair.*

—*brother.*

big sister says

anyone who truly cares for you
won't express themselves
in knuckles, fists, or cruelty.

none of it is normal.

most of all,
i need you to know that
none of it is ever deserved.

"you'd be so much prettier if . . ."
"you'll never get a boyfriend if you don't . . ."

—*what they all tell her.*

big sister says

if you don't want to
shave your legs,
then don't shave your legs.

if you don't want to
wear makeup,
then don't wear makeup.

if you don't want to
get dressed up,
then don't get dressed up.

be the *you*
that is the most comfortable.

her parents screamed at her
more than they ever
told her they loved her.

—*disappointment.*

big sister says

we are not defined by the love our family could or could not give us. we are defined, instead, by the people we consciously become in spite of them—the kindness we show others, the forgiveness we give to ourselves, the times we speak up instead of choosing to remain silent, & the difficult yet necessary apologies we make.

they say never to play favorites with your children because the least favorite will forever be doomed to see themselves as second-best, & it will be a next-to-impossible feat to persuade them otherwise.

—*she knows this from experience.*

big sister says

even if you aren't their favorite,
you're always *someone's* favorite.

(you're mine.)

alone in her bedroom
she declares,

"i'll never be
as *beautiful* as her."

"i'll never be
as *thin* as her."

"i'll never be
as *kind* as her."

"i'll never be
as *beloved* as her."

"i'll never be
as *deserving* as her."

—signed, the ugly sister.

big sister says

sisters shouldn't be
pitting themselves against each other.

sisters should be
going into battle for one another.

the only time
a boy ever
asks her out
is for a laugh.

after so long,
she begins
to see herself
as a joke, too.

—*punch line.*

big sister says

some people feel good about themselves only when they're putting other people down. by making you feel inferior, they, in turn, feel superior. don't give them the satisfaction of a response; give them only dignified silence. trolls belong under bridges, but you, a mighty queen, belong in the castle they can only dream of living in.

"why doesn't anyone want me?"

—*why, why, why?*

big sister says

every girl is trying to survive in a gruesome world that tells her she can never be good enough no matter what she does. rest assured, there is nothing wrong with you, nor has there ever been, so don't you dare try to change anything about yourself. anyone deserving of you will see that you're already worth more than any diamond.

she wants a life
like you see in movies—

the kind where
the girl finally
takes off her glasses,
revealing her true beauty,

& suddenly
she's admired by everybody.

—*she doesn't realize she's already beautiful.*

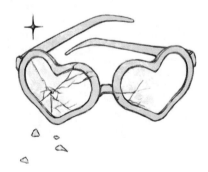

big sister says

there will *always* be a new mascara. there will *always* be a new lipstick. there will *always* be a new pair of jeans. there will *always* be a new ideal body shape. by the time you've finally caught up, there will already be a new trend. it's meant to be unobtainable, because that ensures you'll have no choice but to keep investing your time, money, & energy. respect yourself enough not to buy into a system whose success depends on making you feel insecure. instead, become devoted to being unapologetically yourself.

whenever she's in a room filled with people, she can't help but to feel like she doesn't belong there. most of the time, she doesn't think she has anything worthwhile to say, so she stays in the corner & keeps to herself. if she ever *does* muster up the courage to speak her mind, either nobody bothers to hear her, or they talk right over her. they were always louder, always much more confident than she.

—*wallflower.*

big sister says

don't you dare
undervalue yourself.

don't you dare
become smaller to
make room for others.

don't you dare
shrink back
into the shadows.

don't you dare
wither while
everyone else blooms.

here's an indisputable fact:
you matter.

she's so quiet that
no one ever thinks twice
before spilling
other people's secrets
in front of her—

little do they know
that she's an
excellent listener
& they're teaching her
that no one can
be trusted.

—*traitors.*

big sister says

be mindful of the apples people try to offer you. some will be perfectly delicious, but others may be laced with poison. try not to settle for their toxicity just because you're starving & you think there's nothing better out there for you. the pain you will have to endure isn't worth it. go on—explore new orchards, & don't be afraid to be picky about it. you, my dear, deserve only the sweetest things life has to offer.

her favorite pastime is sitting in coffee shops & imagining the relationships she might have with complete strangers—the hot chocolate they might sip, the snow angels they might make, the sweaters she might steal & declare her own. it's so much easier than having the real thing. this way, they can't reject her, like she knows they would.

—*this way, she never gets hurt.*

big sister says

you are less alone
than you realize.

the trick is to
open your heart

as wide as
a butterfly net.

stay patient—
stay vigilant—

& you will
find your people.

"come to the party."
—*her friends, trying to include her.*

"i'd much rather stay home & get lost in a book."
—*her, running away scared again.*

big sister says

you want so badly
for others to prove that
they care about you,

yet you continue
to push everyone away.

why?

open every window.
let love inside.

it's time you stopped
letting your what-ifs
limit you so much.

kneeling in front of the toilet, she searches for her release. there is nothing in this life she feels she has control over, but this— this *is* something that she can control, & she won't ever let anyone take it away from her.

—*scabs on knuckles.*

big sister says

show gratitude to
one part of you every single day.

if you have legs,
thank them for carrying you.

if you have arms,
thank them for lifting you.

if you have a stomach,
thank it for filling you.

if you have eyes,
thank them for showing you.

if you have a mouth,
thank it for nourishing you.

it's time you reconciled
with your one & only body.

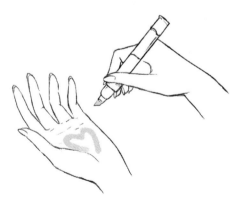

every night she hears
a small, persistent voice
that tries to convince her that

no one has ever felt
as sad or as lonely
or as insignificant

as she does right now.

—*snow princess.*

big sister says

our minds can often feel like a fortress from which we have little hope of escaping. it's very good at making you think that things have always been this way & can never get better, but it can get better, & it will. there is a beginning, a middle, & an end to every single book, & some books even have sequels. you're only at the beginning of the very first book. give the rest of your story a fair chance to unfold.

she wants someone she can have deep conversations with. she wants someone who will take her out for ice cream at one o'clock in the morning. she wants someone she can watch disney movies with when she's sick. she wants someone who will listen to what she has to say without thinking she's either stupid or annoying. she wants someone—*anyone*—to take the time to understand her.

—*is that even possible?*

big sister says

because if you can't

let your hair down
& take your shoes off
& make silly faces

when you're with them,
what's the point?

some days even the idea of getting out of bed seems impossible to her, & she once thought every impossible thing was possible: enchanted furniture, talking animals, invisible friends come to life, breath-giving kisses, faeries, & perhaps the most impossible thing of all, happiness.

—*where did she go?*

big sister says

anything
you're brave enough
to believe in
is more than possible.

don't start small.

begin with
your wildest dreams.

accept nothing less.
nothing.

her depression
makes her anxious

&

her anxiety
makes her depressed.

—*never-ending.*

big sister says

be as courageous
as i know you can be.

fight on.
fight on, wolf-heart.

canceled plans
make her sigh in relief.

—*now she won't have to fake it.*

big sister says

remember this:
it is okay not to be okay.

cry it out,
write it all down,
scream it into a pillow.

tell somebody.

allow yourself to feel
however it is that you feel—

honor your emotions
so you can finally be set free.

her friends never seem to understand that she can't be there for them when she hasn't even learned how to properly be there for herself. instead of empathizing with her, they accuse her of being *selfish*.

—*hurt*.

big sister says

a true friend
understands when
you aren't able to
show up for them.

an even better friend
understands when
you have to show up
for yourself instead.

if they refuse to,
then i hope you can see that
they were never actually
your friend.

she closes her eyes
& makes the same silent wish:

i will not wake up tomorrow.
i will not wake up tomorrow.
i will not wake up tomorrow.

—she's not sure anyone is listening.

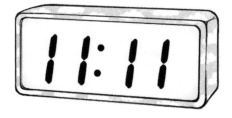

big sister says

one morning you'll wake up before the sun has a chance to rise & see the moonbeams slanting through your bedroom window, & despite every bad thing that's ever happened to you, you'll feel well rested & excited to see what new adventures await you. you'll realize just how fucking grateful you are that you decided to stay alive to experience this quiet, wonderful moment. this i can promise you.

yet again, someone asks her what's wrong, & she assures them that she feels fine; she's just tired. "i didn't get much sleep last night," she says. it always feels like she's lying to everyone around her, but she isn't. she *is* tired—not just physically but also mentally & emotionally.

—*perfecting her excuses.*

big sister says

challenge #1:

start telling the truth
when someone asks you
how you're doing.

challenge #2:

ask more questions
when someone says they're fine
& you know they're lying.

let's normalize
caring about each other—
not out of politeness

but out of genuine
human compassion.

no,

hurting herself
is *not* something she
does for the attention.

some days,

it's the only thing
that tethers her
to the earth.

—*she feels like she might float away any day now.*

big sister says

they will try to convince you that you have no right to be unhappy—that other people have it so much worse than you do. even if that last statement is true, *it doesn't matter.* your pain is yours, & comparing it to the pain of others doesn't solve the problem. do not let their words stop you from reaching out for the help you need.

she begins to think something very, very dangerous: maybe, just *maybe*, she'll find the happiness she wants if she loses herself in someone else.

—*reckless.*

big sister says

love is not
always the answer.

it is not a cure-all,
nor should it ever
replace therapy.

allow your partner to be
a fallible human being,
a source of support.

not your everything.

the more boys she kisses,
the more she realizes that
she has much more
interesting things to do.

—*she wonders whether something is wrong with her.*

big sister says

it's perfectly okay if what you want for yourself isn't what other people want for you. this is *your* fairy tale, darling—you're the only one who has to live it, so you're the only one who has to be happy with it.

she's so tired of men
telling her how strong she is.

—*she already knows.*

big sister says

she hates the thought of settling down with one person right now, & they tell her that makes her far less valuable—*a lock with far too many keys.*

—*slut-shaming.*

big sister says

if you were a man,
you'd be allowed
to date as many women
as you wanted.

you'd never even
be questioned;
in fact, you'd be
celebrated like a god.

do not for
one single minute
put up with these
double standards.

they open doors for her. they pull out seats for her. they pay for her dinner. they give her their jackets when she forgets her own. proudly, they claim it's all in the name of being a so-called *gentleman,* but she can't help but feel like they don't think she's capable.

—*there isn't a single thing she can't do for herself.*

big sister says

you are your own empress.
you are your own high priestess.
you are your own goddess.

your independence
will intimidate some—
it may even offend others.

let it.

that's their own problem,
not yours.

"you're too pretty to be single."
—*he.*

"i'm too pretty to even talk to you."
—*she.*

big sister says

there's nothing wrong with seeing the immensity of your worth. there's nothing wrong with acting self-assured. there's nothing wrong with demanding the respect you deserve. walk with your head held up so high that you can't even see the peasants beneath you.

eventually, she starts having to tell men that she's happily taken by another, resenting the fact that it's the only boundary they ever seem to respect.

—*wearing a fake ring.*

big sister says

if he throws a tantrum
when you tell him "no"—

if he tries to guilt you
when you tell him "no"—

if he tries to force you
when you tell him "no"—

know that you
do not owe him shit.

her sister introduces
her boyfriend,

but all she can see is
a man who looks at women
like they're his prey.

"you *better* treat her right,"
she warns him.

—*the huntsman.*

big sister says

one of the most challenging things you can do is see someone you love making decisions that you know will hurt them. we can speak from a place of experience & try to talk some sense into them, but they have the free will not to listen to us, & they so often don't. there isn't much you can do except be there for them, no matter what.

when her heart breaks,
hers breaks even harder,
so she takes karma
into her own hands.

—*revenge.*

big sister says

i'm beginning to realize that sisters are in your life forever, while lovers usually stay in our lives only but for a moment in time. honor the fellow women in your life every single chance you get. check in on them. offer them a shoulder or two. lay roses at their feet. make sure they know that they're never truly alone, because they have you.

she refuses to be *only*
someone else's daughter.

she refuses to be *only*
someone else's sister.

she refuses to be *only*
someone else's girlfriend.

she refuses to be *only*
someone else's wife.

she refuses to be *only*
someone else's mother.

—*her potential knows no bounds.*

big sister says

make them rue the day they underestimated you.

ii

the princess never found a crown she was happy with. throughout the years, she continued to dismiss every single one a man tried to place upon her head, even handsome princes with tempting promises of marriage & riches. in return, they called her horrible things: *cold*, *heartless*, & her personal favorite, *frigid*. eventually, she decided to craft one of her own—a magnificent piece made from ice-like crystals, the very first of its kind. when she was done, the points were so sharp they could wound a man if he got too near. this only made the hatred for the princess grow. she no longer cried about it at night; instead, she smiled, completely unaffected, & shined her crown until it sparkled. *growth.*

she always looked up to
strong women protagonists—

that is, until the day
she finally realized that
she is the strong woman protagonist.

determined is she
to weave an even better tale.

—taking the pen back.

you say *lonely.*

i say *self-sufficient.*
i say *content dating myself.*

—*your local spinster.*

when a mere dusting of snow covers the streets, there are entire cities that shut down because they aren't prepared for the danger it brings. that won't be me. the winter of my life *cannot* & *will not* triumph over me, for i decided a long time ago that defeat is not a choice worth considering.

—*the definition of a fighter.*

i'm not doomed to repeat
my parents' mistakes,

or my parents'
parents' mistakes,

or my parents' parents'
parents' mistakes.

—*i'm not even doomed to repeat my own mistakes.*

telling you that i don't plan on having any children is not an attack on your choices or your dreams. just as well, it's not an opportunity for you to tell me that i'll change my mind when i finally meet the right person. maybe i *will* change my mind, but it's just as possible that i *won't*.

—*my fate is not a forgone conclusion.*

if i decide to be with you,
it's not because
i think you *complete* me.

i'm already a complete
spiritual being
without anybody's help.

if i'm with you,
it's because i think you
let in more stardust than storm clouds.

—*what i look for.*

yes, i am one of those awful bra-burning feminists. no, i do not hate all men. no, i do not want to switch out the patriarchy for a matriarchy. what i do want, however, is complete equality—a fair chance at becoming the best version of myself. no more restrictions.

less girl-on-girl hate.
more group protection spells.

—*solidarity.*

if your feminism comes to a screeching halt whenever you don't like how tightly her dress hugs her curves or the way she does her own makeup, then stop to consider this: are you *actually* a feminist?

—*do better.*

stop judging a woman on
whether or not she takes
her spouse's last name.

if she changes it,
that doesn't mean she's
suddenly their property.

if she doesn't change it,
it doesn't mean she's
superior to those who do.

her decision,
her business.

—doesn't she deal with enough already?

teach your daughter
that her value
is never tied to the
number of people
she has or has not
slept with.

wear the term "basic bitch"
with a sense of pride.

embrace every part of you
they told you to hate.

—unbothered.

when we empower ourselves, we inspire others to empower themselves. step up & lead the way for others to follow in your footsteps. encourage them to do better than you were able to, because hope can never be lost as long as the future rests in the hands of our sisters & siblings.

—*be the light.*

do not wait until someone
tells you that you can—
we made it this far only because
we decided that we could.

—minds of our very own.

"women can't rule;
they're far too emotional."

*but isn't it about time
someone actually cared?*

they fear women leaders
the same way they fear
an impending hurricane.

both are determined—
both are merciless.

we will not stop fighting
until we change the entire
landscape they created.

—*persist | always.*

let's go ahead & take back the term "snowflake," for it's never been about wanting to get some kind of special treatment we haven't earned. all we want is for the world to finally see the complexities of the magic that lies within each & every one of us & respect it accordingly.

—*it's not that difficult.*

she isn't trying to impress you.
she's trying to impress *herself.*

go to the movies & see a rom-com by yourself. go to your favorite restaurant & request a table for one. go to a café & order a coffee & a pastry for yourself. lie in the grass & cloudgaze without holding someone else's hand while you do it. we need to stop seeing these things as pathetic. you are the only person you have to be with every day, so why shouldn't you find ways to appreciate *you*?

—*keep falling in love with yourself.*

fearless is she.

to them, this means that
she is a dangerous thing,

because they have no hope
of ever taming her.

—*she would have it no other way.*

i'm afraid i don't have time to go into the kitchen & make you a sandwich—you see, i already have my hands full, for i'm busy saving the world.

—my sincerest apologies.

the only one stopping you
from holding the moon
in your own two hands

is *you*.

—*self-limiting beliefs.*

mulheres.

—*esse é o poema.*

mulheres.

—*esse é o poema.*

mothers are amazing—

there's no question
about it.

but keep in mind
that motherhood
is not the only way
to be amazing.

—*for anyone who needs to hear it.*

they tell us to fear nothing more than growing old, but you know what i think? *fuck that.* i, for one, cannot wait to get grey hair, crow's feet, & sun spots. if men get to be silver foxes, then we get to be the old wise crones with vast, otherworldly knowledge.

—aging should be a celebration.

even though i know you can,
you need not take on
everything at once.

show yourself some
kindness.

take off your armor.
put away your sword.
lay each of your arrows down.

i promise
it can wait until tomorrow.

—it's time to rest.

don't be scared to trust, but don't take that to mean that you need to trust every single soul you meet on your journey— that's naive, not to mention unsafe. it's good to be on guard sometimes, for not everyone has your best interests at heart. get to a point where it's enough for you to have those few loyal people who stand beneath the tightrope ready to catch you if & when you slip.

—*minimalism.*

as painful as it may be,
it is always easier to
walk away from the villain

than it is to try to
convince them of their villainy.

—*a hard pill to swallow.*

i've been spending
more nights at home.

i've been reading
my horoscope.

i've been turning off
my phone.

i've been minding
my own business.

i've been aligning
with my true self.

—*why you haven't heard from me lately.*

i'm no longer leaving
space for anyone who
doesn't seek to uplift me.

i'm no longer leaving
space for anyone who
uses me for their own gain
& throws me away when
i no longer benefit them.

i'm no longer leaving
space for anyone whose
presence does nothing
but block my flow of light.

—*you are henceforth banished.*

no more fake friends.
no more following the crowd.
no more hiding my feelings.

no more pretending.

—*authenticity only.*

find pride in every version of you
that has ever existed.

they saw you through so much.
they are what got you here.

& the *you* that's reading this now
will be the reason why

future you has gotten to
even more incredible places.

—*every chapter serves you.*

embody the heroine you needed when you were a child, but don't forget to embody the heroine you need *now*, too.

—*nurture all of you.*

i. drive the scenic route.
ii. take more self-care days.
iii. sing, even if it's off-key.
iv. make time for your passions.
v. let yourself feel joy.

—*don't waste a single moment.*

i used to think that crying made me seem hysterical or fragile, but now i know that allowing myself to be vulnerable is, above all, a superpower very few possess.

—*the flood that frees me.*

standing in my power
doesn't stop me from
experiencing self-doubt,

just as experiencing self-doubt
doesn't stop me from
standing in my power.

—balancing act.

taking care of your needs
when you have no motivation to.

—*small magic.*

i've learned not to let it upset me when someone points out my scars & questions how they came to be. years ago, i might have made up a terrible excuse or tried to escape. now i tell them, "thank you so much for noticing. they are the indisputable proof that i have not only *lived* but prospered despite every odd that was ever against me."

—*a modern fairy tale.*

it is your divine right
to heal as messily
& as inconsistently
& as loudly as possible.

i hereby swear to own
every single one of my actions,
even if they are caused by
the state of my mental health.

it may be a reason,
but it is *never* an excuse.

—a promise to myself.

choosing softness is not a fault or a weakness. sometimes the most valiant thing you can do is make the choice to focus on the beauty left among all this ruination.

i deserve to have good things
even if i have not always
done good things.

—perfection is a lie; flaws are real.

"i will be ever patient with myself,
because i am worth putting time & care into."

—*morning mantra.*

journey as far outside
of your comfort zone
as you can possibly go.

evolve so magnificently
that you make even
butterflies jealous.

take risk
after risk
after risk.

—*the rebirth.*

do not plan your life
so meticulously that
you leave no space
for starlight to leak in.

—*miracles happen only if you let them.*

recently, i've been doing some shadow work. i'm no longer hiding from painful memories; instead, i'm fully embracing them & learning from every lesson they have to teach me. which is to say that everything that once nearly destroyed me is now what lights my path forward, & i think that's exceptional.

in fact, i think i am exceptional.

—a love letter to myself.

iii

the princess who wore a crown of her own making stood tall, her hands on her hips & her chin pointed to the sky. the crowd was completely silent as she began to speak. whether it was out of fear or out of respect, she wasn't quite sure. "screw the outdated tradition. i don't need to have a king in order to be called a queen. i have always been a queen in my own right, & now i'm officially declaring it, so bow down," & so they did, without question.

—her unconventional happily ever after.

special acknowledgments

i. *my spouse, cyrus parker*—thank you for all that you do, especially the inspiring cups of matcha you make. <3

ii. *janaina medeiros*—thank you for the lovely art! this book & this series wouldn't be the same without it.

iii. *christine day & mira kennedy*—thank you for helping me be a better writer, even if you don't always agree with each other! ;)

iv. *gabriela castro*—thank you so much for your valuable feedback!

v. *my family*—thank you for always believing in me.

vi. *my readers*—thank you for going on journey after journey with me.

about the author

amanda lovelace is the author of several bestselling poetry titles, including her celebrated "women are some kind of magic" trilogy as well as her new "you are your own fairy tale" series. she is also the co-creator of the *believe in your own magic* oracle deck. when she isn't reading, writing, or drinking a much-needed cup of coffee, you can find her casting spells from her home in a (very) small town on the jersey shore, where she resides with her poet-spouse & their three cats.

follow the author

 @ladybookmad

 @ladybookmad

 amandalovelace.com

Andrews McMeel Publishing
a division of Andrews McMeel Universal
1130 Walnut Street, Kansas City, Missouri 64106

www.andrewsmcmeel.com

21 22 23 24 25 RR2 10 9 8 7 6 5 4 3 2 1

ISBN: 978-1-5248-5194-1

Library of Congress Control Number: 2020945912

Illustrations by Janaina Medeiros

Editor: Patty Rice
Art Director/Designer: Julie Barnes
Production Editor: Dave Shaw
Production Manager: Cliff Koehler